CROSS MARKETING

Here's Your Wake Up Call

Marlin R. Bollinger

authorHOUSE®

AuthorHouse™
1663 Liberty Drive
Bloomington, IN 47403
www.authorhouse.com
Phone: 1-800-839-8640

First published by AuthorHouse   6/9/2011

ISBN: 978-1-4634-1509-9 (sc)
ISBN: 978-1-4634-1511-2 (e)

Library of Congress Control Number: 2011908616

Printed in the United States of America

Any people depicted in stock imagery provided by Thinkstock are models, and such images are being used for illustrative purposes only. Certain stock imagery © Thinkstock.

This book is printed on acid-free paper.

To my wife, Pattra,
whose love, understanding, and constant subjection to hypothetical questions (she retired from the P/C business) helped me to comprehend another side of the insurance business.

Preface

This book is the result of years of hard work by professionals on both the financial services side and the property/casualty side of the business. The evolution, or lack thereof, of cross marketing in the property/casualty and banking industries has been an arduous and ongoing work in progress. Many have tried with minimal success, while a small percentage has overwhelmingly succeeded. I consider this book a must-read for those who have not achieved their cross-marketing goals, those who have not taken cross marketing seriously in the past, and those who choose to thrive in this decade. This is it Here's your wake up call!

Introduction

Marketing insurance products in the next ten years will present new challenges for the property/casualty, institutional, and independent life agent. Retail agents in all disciplines must understand the evolution of insurance marketing and distribution. Many agents think the challenge is to survive; I think the challenge is to thrive. Mere survival may be acceptable for many, but those at the head of the pack will realize the rewards of evolutionary success, and they will thrive!

This book is not necessarily a "how to" manual of contemporary selling and marketing strategies. It is intended to be a thought-provoking chronology of our evolution from the late '70s into 2010 and beyond. We can and should have learned from the past, but so many of us do not fit the final pieces into the puzzle until it's too late. The beauty in a puzzle is that once you've constructed the outline, the pieces don't necessarily have to be put together in any special order. They just have to eventually all fit together.

Although hindsight may be 20/20, trends and business functions are cyclical. If the P/C market is hard, it's only a matter of time until it again softens. At this writing, things are very soft and getting softer. What goes down must go back up, and vice versa. Profit margins are under immense pressure, consolidation is rampant, costs are being shifted from company to agency, and commissions and contingencies are being slashed. To some, these challenges may seem ominous, requiring a herculean effort to recover. To others, these facts present an exciting opportunity. They see an opportunity to grow and meld the proven methods of insurance sales and services with the technologies of today and tomorrow.

Those of you from the property/casualty persuasion have surely heard, time and time again, the insurance company study directly relating the number of lines sold to customer loyalty and retention. The same study also applies to institutional agents. If the customer only purchased one line of coverage, most of them will be prone to investigate the competitive marketplace on a regular basis. Lock in more lines, and your retention percentage increases.

In an article published in the *P&C National Underwriter* on November 25, 2008, author Shirley Woods writes,

> "As traditional sources of property-casualty revenue remain relatively flat, the most successful agencies are navigating this period of slow growth by finding new sources of business. They are looking to stock their proverbial "shelves" with an expanded array of new insurance coverage and financial products for their clients."

A natural segue is into the marketing of financial services. Life insurance, annuity, and certain health insurance products are being purchased by their clients on a regular basis. If the casualty agency does not approach the client with these products, someone else will. Organic growth through the sale of life insurance and related products makes perfect sense for the agency. Not only will it boost their top and bottom lines, but it will also serve as a great retention strategy.

Cost wise, growth through the sale of additional product lines to existing clients is substantially more cost effective that growth through acquisition. It always amazes me when an inexperienced agency hires a "life guy". One of the first mistakes they make is to assume the "life guy" is bringing a book of business with him. After they realize that the book of business is insignificant, they look to the purchase of outside leads, never realizing that they have a goldmine in their own book of clients.

It is interesting to note that most clients would rather purchase their financial services products through their property-casualty agent, assuming the agent or agency is qualified. Clients would rather deal with a single agency or producer for all their insurance and financial needs.

Many agencies have a natural fear of marketing financial services products. They are concerned about their lack of knowledge regarding these products and the marketing concepts associated with them. Most property-casualty agencies have a mix of personal and commercial clients. Most commercial accounts are small business owners, highly dependent upon good advice from the agents that serve them. Many BGA's offer more than just products. They offer help with product and marketing presentations as well as point of sale assistance. Most successful property-casualty agencies have become successful in cross-selling by utilizing someone else's talent via the "assisted sale". We'll talk more about that later in the book.

It really all comes down to developing a workable marketing plan and trust. The marketing plan must be solid, comprehensive, and totally customized for the agency. Although there a few "rules of thumb", every agency is unique. The consulting entity must have the full faith and trust of the property-casualty agency to achieve truly meaningful results.

Although Ms. Woods's article is timely, it may well have been written over a decade ago. Honestly, progress has been slow, even in a sustained "soft" market. It would be unfair to attempt to identify one specific reason, but the transactional, reactive nature of the P/C business has certainly contributed to this procrastination. It is the opinion of this author that quite often, the lack of action should not be thrown on the P/C agency, but on the poorly devised marketing systems offered to the P/C agencies by a myriad of companies and quasi-self-proclaimed financial services professionals.

There is still time for those who choose to thrive in the coming decade to do so. They must, however, have a firm knowledge of the history of our industry, both property casualty and other financial services. And, most importantly, they must align themselves with a firm that is historically reputable and totally committed to the total cross-marketing package.

Although the highway of cross-selling programs and services is strewn with past failures, Ms. Wood got it right when she referred to a decidedly sunny outlook. The cross-marketing professionals on the financial services side of the business understand that a huge window of opportunity is currently open.

Industry visionary Edward W. Cassidy is heading a new initiative by the Phoenix Companies. The new company, Saybrus Partners Inc., was founded on the premise that national financial services companies still want to cross sell life insurance products to their clients. According to Cassidy, the managing principal at Saybrus, Cross-selling is going to continue to be a big driver of business for banks, broker-dealers, and property/casualty companies in terms of adding revenue to the bottom line. Client retention will also continue to be critical. By helping these companies cross-sell, they can get more of a client's wallet and have the opportunity to keep these customers.

Initiating a "call to action" is the essence of this book. Front and center, this is your wake up call!

CHAPTER 1

How It All Started

It was April of 1978, and I had just concluded a short consulting stint at a radio station in Springfield, Massachusetts. After two previous false starts in Florida, I was determined to make this one stick. Unfortunately, there were no radio programming positions open, and my funds were rapidly dwindling. So, like so many others, I entered the insurance industry by accident. I needed a job, and the career companies were hiring. I became a life insurance man. At that time, the quintessential life insurance agent represented only one company and sold but a few simple products, either whole life or renewable and convertible term. We also had a small arsenal of disability, annuity, and individual and group medical products. But we mostly focused on life insurance sales.

My first company was the Equitable Life Assurance Society of America, the Equitable. There were two distinct sales divisions: DSF and ESF. The DSF (developing sales force) agents were the neophytes, and the ESF agents were experienced. I never made it to the ESF division. Neither did over 90 percent of the other DSFs. In spite of that fact, I was one of the more successful DSF agents. My success was attributable to being able to sell insurance to my family, my friends, and a reasonable number of solicited prospects.

Like so many other previously staid institutions, the insurance industry was beginning to change in the '70s. As Robert Littell and Larry McSpadden so aptly describe in their book, *Crossing the Line*, "A career as a 'life agent' was viewed by many as a 'calling'—carrying out the obviously altruistic work of protecting future widows and orphans from poverty and despair. Top life agents were highly visible people within their communities, participating in fraternal, civic, and charitable organizations. With little negative media focus, the life agent was admired; media questions regarding the life product's competitive value or intrinsic worth were never heard. No one criticized the life agent's or company's marketing practices."[1]

To survive in those early years, I regularly returned to my hometown in Pennsylvania to call on those folks I knew and grew up with. That was a lot easier than the cold calls required to survive in southern Florida. It was also substantially more productive. Unfortunately, there are only so many people you can call upon in a small rural town of only ten thousand. Nevertheless, it kept the wheels moving while I attempted to define the prospecting techniques that worked for me at home.

Most career shops required their new agents to conduct Monday-night calls. Those calls were directly from the phone book, reciting a predetermined script written by the training department of the respective company. "Cold" may not be the appropriate term; perhaps "frozen" is better. The sessions normally lasted for up to three hours or until we were totally exhausted or were fortunate enough to schedule ten appointments for the week. Bottom line, it wasn't for me.

What worked for me was cold calling small businesses for group insurance. If the business had a plan, they were usually interested in saving premiums at their renewals. If I could get to the owners, I could usually interest them in providing a competitive quote. In the late '70s and early '80s, small group plans in Florida were often guaranteed issue with no loss/no gain. That made it easy to replace their present plans with more competitive plans. Although it was a much better prospecting method compared to the Monday-night calling sessions, it was still quite difficult. Once I wrote the group plan, I asked to review their business and personal insurance portfolios.

After my subsidy was about to expire at the Equitable, it was off to State Mutual for a new round of financing. Although I appeared to be successful, the career companies were really providing an overly aggressive financing program, in hopes of supporting the new agents until such time as they became self-supportive. It was quite common for agents to move from company to company just to get refinanced. I was no exception.

At State Mutual, I was educated in the business and estate-planning markets and became quite proficient at creating my own usable models for presentation. Of course, compliance had a completely different meaning in 1980 than it does today. My presentation and creative organizational skills soon became known among the less-experienced agents, and my career in insurance was solidified. The new agents were capable of scheduling the required weekly appointments but fell a bit short of sales and presentation acumen. I was able to validate my contract by making joint sales calls and splitting cases.

I soon realized the power of knowledge and persuasion. I'd let the other agents do the heavy lifting, while I prepared the presentations and made the sale. I'm sure these new agents considered me the heavy lifter, since they did not have the confidence to close. I found the business plan that worked for me!

Having transitioned from a very creative management position in the radio and advertising industry to insurance sales may seem somewhat unconventional. In fact, it was just the opposite. Creative concepting is one of the keystones to success in both advertising and insurance. The fundamentals are essentially the same. If you can successfully bring a product to market or grow a radio audience by developing a more listened-to format, you can develop creative marketing systems in the insurance industry. The only difference is that you must first develop the technical expertise and product knowledge to guide you through the creative marketing process.

My success with joint sales certainly simplified my prospecting dilemma but didn't satisfy my desire to reenter management, this time in insurance.

It made good sense to seek a sales management position, considering the reality of receiving an override for the production of those agents under my management. If I could make joint sales, then I could certainly develop and train others to do the same. The more successful agents I trained, the more successful I would be—or so I thought. So off I went to interview for a sales management position and found one rather quickly. The offer was from Home Life, a New York company claiming to have the highest percentage of CLUs in the industry. But, somehow, I got sidetracked and accepted an interview with the Travelers.

The Travelers interview was somewhat foreign, in that I didn't really get their plan. The position was that of a production supervisor. The role of a production supervisor was a jack-of-all-trades sales job that focused around the agencies appointed by the Travelers to market property/casualty insurance. I would be working for a department of a larger property/casualty insurance company. How was I supposed to sell life insurance and related products to clients of these agencies?

I accepted the position at Home Life. When I called the Travelers manager to inform him of my decision, he put a full-court press on me to reconsider. Not only would I get a company car, but I would also have a healthy expense account, neither of which was offered by Home Life. Although I still didn't fully understand how Travelers could build a profitable business model, I decided to give it a chance.

CHAPTER 2

The Travelers

To be specific, it was the Travelers Life, Health, and Financial Services Department, LHFS for short. The Travelers LHFS was managed by region. The Fort Lauderdale office was part of the southern region, domiciled in Atlanta. The personnel structure was quite impressive. Working out of the regional office with the regional vice president were two estate planning specialists, one tax sheltered annuity specialist, and one payroll deduction specialist. Add to that their administrative staff. In the local office, we had a marketing manager, four production supervisors/managers, and five administrative coordinators.

Each production supervisor/manager was responsible for a unit of agents/agencies. We were free to contract any licensed agent, but the bulk of our production came directly from those agencies contracted through the property/casualty department. Although my goal was to evolve into a management position, I soon realized that the Travelers position was very similar to the joint sales situation I had left behind at State Mutual. At the Travelers, I was trained to market a portfolio of stock company products: non-par whole life, blended non-par whole life, term insurance, and annuity riders to compete with participating dividend scales. Both Equitable and State Mutual were mutual companies, offering dividend paying participating whole life contracts.

Most property/casualty agencies in the early '80s were relatively small family-owned businesses. Many of these agencies were heavily weighted in personal lines with a small volume of BOP policies on the commercial side. Total premium generated was, on average, somewhere in the one- to three-million-dollar range. Of course, there were larger agencies where the commercial volume dominated their personal lines volume. Most of these agencies also produced their P/C business with either the Travelers, the Aetna, or the Hartford. They were the big three!

Each of the big three had some kind of financial services department, and all wanted as much as they could get from their contracted agencies. Fortunately, the Travelers had more staff dedicated to financial services production than the other two combined. Product-wise, we were all offering similar products of mediocre quality. That's where the similarity ended.

The Travelers realized early on that some form of value added was necessary to realize success with these multiline agencies. Here's how we did it.

Production supervisors were required to call on all Travelers multiline agencies on a regular basis. Most of the agencies did not have a life department and relied solely on the principal and the other producers to write the business. Or, let me say, sign the application as agent. Well, that's not entirely correct. Quite often, the production supervisors were the sales agents soliciting the applications, and we signed for the listed agents. We did not forge their names on the applications but merely signed for them: for example, John Jones (production supervisor) for James Smith (agent). That procedure would not be permissible in today's more compliant industry. Quite often, the agent never saw the client, just referred them to the production supervisor via a telephone call. The production supervisor booked the appointment, ascertained the need, made the sale, and, many times, delivered the policy. The agent simply made the referral.

Not all production supervisors were successful. The successful supervisors realized early on that the ability to form a relationship with the agency was equally as important, if not more so, than their product knowledge or sales skills. We really got to know our agents, their agencies, and their employees. We worked so closely that we were often considered part of the agency and invited to employee-only functions. We became part of the agency family.

Molding a solid business relationship with an agency principal is not as simple as it may seem. One of the most difficult tasks in developing a successful production relationship is trust. *Merriam-Webster Online* defines "trust" as "assured reliance on the character, ability, strength, or truth of someone or something."[2] The successful production supervisor formed a bond of trust with several multiline agencies.

Prior to being introduced to our agency force, we were thoroughly trained in several areas: product offerings of the company, understanding the competition, style awareness, property/casualty jargon, and a proven sales track. We tagged along with the more experienced production managers until we felt comfortable in a multiline environment.

While all this training was in progress, we were also introduced to our counterparts on the Travelers property/casualty side of the business. That part of the training was more informal but extremely valuable. We learned about each agency, its mix of business, and the issues faced from a P/C perspective.

Remember the structure of the company as previously discussed? The local office was supported on a regional level by several specialists. These specialists were constantly on the road supporting the sales efforts of the local offices in the region. Not only did we have a strong local face presence with our agencies, but a highly qualified regional backup team to physically support our advanced sales efforts. Imagine a small personal lines P/C agency being able to provide sophisticated estate analysis services to their clientele. We're not just talking concept here but a fully customized estate plan, presented by a highly qualified professional.

THE SALES TRACK

The Travelers sales track consisted of three parts: the Ben Duffy, the human asset risk analysis, and the appropriate subsequent presentation. All production supervisors were taught to commit to memory the entire sales track and to present all aspects of the track to their agencies on a regular basis.

Advertising icon Ben Duffy joined the advertising firm of BBDO circa

1931 as a clerk in the mailroom. Ben worked his way up the ranks of the Madison Avenue firm, achieving its presidency in 1946. Duffy was an excellent salesman who could close a deal quickly. When Foote, Cone, and Belding resigned the eleven-million-dollar American Tobacco Company account in 1948, Duffy went directly to see American Tobacco's George Hill and secured the account after one meeting. In Duffy's ten years at the helm of BBDO, the agency increased its billings from fifty million dollars to over two hundred million dollars. Story has it that on the way to the appointment, Mr. Duffy wrote down as many questions as he could think of that might be on the prospect's mind. He narrowed the questions to ten. Thus, the birth of the Ben Duffy method: selling from a customer's perspective.

THE BEN DUFFY METHOD

The concept is simple: put yourself in the shoes of the prospect and think of the questions he or she will ask prior to making a decision. Whenever production supervisors met a client of an agency for the first time, they presented their version of the Ben Duffy. It went something like this: "On my way to the appointment today, I thought of some questions you might ask of me." Those questions are the following:

1. Who am I?
2. Why am I here?
3. How do I do business?

Your Ben Duffy introduction had previously been reviewed with the principal of the agency you were representing. The principal knew exactly what you were going to say to his or her client. The Ben Duffy, and the human asset risk analysis and appropriate subsequent presentation were the first two steps in a seven-step process called the sales development system (SDS).

The seven-step SDS comprised an entire selling process. It included two separate problem-solving presentations. The first was the money-planning presentation, designed for the estate-planning prospect. It was, however, an all-purpose presentation.

The other one was the business-planning presentation, specifically geared to the wants and needs of the small business owner prospect.

THE RISK ANALYSIS

After providing a brief biographical background, the production supervisor proceeded to explain his or her role within the agency, which led directly into the "How do I do business?" question. Let's assume the production supervisor is meeting with a commercial client of the agency. The risk analysis is perhaps the most important part of the sales track and the SDS. It is most important because it is the part of the SDS that ties the services provided by the P/C agent directly to the services of the financial services representative. Here's the risk analysis presentation:

> Now, in response to that "How do I do business?" question, Ms. Client, let me say that a significant part of my job is to provide clients of the ABC agency with an important service called "human asset risk analysis." Let me explain specifically what that is. All business owners are exposed to risks of almost every description, but those risks really break down into two categories: property risks and human asset risks.

In your dealings with Mr. Jones (the agency P/C salesperson), I know he has carefully explained the property risks you face every day fire, water damage, work interruption, and all the other things that can endanger your company and its operation. In each case, you had a decision to make:

- To cover all of the risk
- To cover part of the risk
- To cover none of the risk

In determining this, you and Mr. Jones worked as a team, and once the risk was analyzed and all the facts were weighed, he helped you select the best course of action for you to take in light of your individual situation.

It is also important to follow that very same risk analysis procedure in another risk area, the human asset side of your business, because that represents an even greater risk to your business than any potential damage to your plant and equipment.

Now, when I speak of the human asset risk, Ms. Client, I'm primarily talking about you. You built this business, you manage it, and you make it run. Without you, it will undergo drastic change and may even cease to exist. And because human beings are mortal, it is a certainty that it must someday operate without you.

When that day comes, Ms. Client, certain things will happen to your business, all of them bad! We feel it is important for these risks to be analyzed and explained to you, along with our recommendations on how to minimize or eliminate them. When we do that, you will have the same decisions to make as you had on the property side:

- To cover all of the risk
- To cover part of the risk
- To cover none of the risk

These decisions are entirely yours to make. Our job is to point out the risks, explain what they are, and give you our recommendations on what should be done about them. Fair enough?

The risk analysis is extremely important for several reasons: It provides the P/C agency principal or agent with a strong comfort level regarding your approach to his or her client. Secondly, it very clearly explains to the agency clients their value to the business and the extensive risks associated with the human asset side of their businesses. Chances are they had never really understood these risks as they were presented. It makes perfect sense for the P/C agency to provide total risk analysis for their valuable clients!

Appropriate Subsequent Presentation

At this stage in the SDS, the production supervisor took one of several directions. If they were presenting to a commercial client of the agency, they would proceed with an explanation of the structure(C-corp., S-corp., LLC, partnership, or sole proprietor) of the business from a taxation point of view. The discussion would focus on reducing the risks presented in a tax-advantaged way.

If the production supervisor was meeting with a personal lines client, he or she would use Tom Wolff's financial or capital needs analysis. You may have seen this presentation in the past, commonly referred to as the funnel talk. Nevertheless, client's assets were divided into four categories: personal assets, business assets, life insurance, and government programs. All four categories flowed into the funnel at death. Expenses were then taken out with the remainder going to the family beneficiaries somewhat similar to the flow of a dollar through a universal life policy.[3]

The Ben Duffy and the risk analysis and appropriate subsequent presentation are the first two steps of the sales development system. Here are all seven in order:

1. Approach
2. Risk Analysis and ASP
3. Data and Priorities
4. Analyze Data and Options
5. Present Solutions
6. Support Action
7. Service and Follow Through

As you can see, the entire process was extremely well thought out. Nothing was left to chance. Quite often, the production supervisor was provided the opportunity to execute the SDS with the principal of the firm he or she was representing. If you'll recall, no presentations were made to clients of the agency prior to being presented to and approved by the agency principal. The reason for this type of approach is obvious in that we wanted the principal to have peace of mind and trust in his or her newest agency representative. By presenting to the principal first, we helped him or her understand exactly what we were doing and recognize the value of the service. But there is another reason for presenting to the principal in advance. Many became their own clients. During their initial presentations, they realized their own personal needs and took action. What better way to develop a deep sense of trust than to offer them these valuable services?

At this point in the relationship, the other P/C companies, vying for the attention of the agencies, were pretty much out in the dark. They continued to call on the agencies but were quite often cornered into a position of weakness and forced to play their trump cards.

THE TRUMP CARD

If we could go back thirty years and ask the agency principals how much life insurance they purchased on family members, we would probably get a very positive response. Family members were usually covered quite well with policies from companies other than the Travelers. I just told you that the agency principals were so impressed with the SDS that they took advantage of the service and became their own clients. Now, I'm telling you that they bought life insurance from the competitors for their entire families. That's where the trump card comes in.

Property/casualty contracts are a valuable entity, and the agencies were willing to do whatever it took to maintain a working P/C relationship with their core companies. Since the financial services divisions of the competitive companies found it difficult to compete with the Travelers on a level playing field, they devised other ways to write the business.

Call it whatever you choose, but the fact is that many companies strongly implied that the agencies would be looked at more favorably if they wrote some life insurance, in addition to the usual P/C coverage. In fact, actual premium numbers were often discussed within specific time frames.

Here's how it usually played out. The companies that presented implied quotas were given what they requested, nothing more. The Travelers wrote substantially more than the competing companies, simply to be providing a value-added service and not employing the trump card approach.

To be fair, the other companies had many qualified and highly trained professionals servicing the agencies. But, by mere numbers alone, they found it difficult to compete with the services offered by the Travelers.

Although I previously referred to the big three, there were other significant companies competing for financial services business at the same time: companies like the St. Paul, CNA, and others. Consolidation had certainly taken its toll in that the Travelers of 2010 is the unification of Travelers, St. Paul, and the Aetna. Who would have predicted that thirty years ago? CNA, perhaps the most aggressive of the trump card players, flat out sold their financial services division to a reinsurer. Thousands of term policy holders of P/C agencies were left high and dry. The new owners had no desire to continue writing new policies and ceased all production. The existing policyholders did have the option to convert, but these options were diluted, in that the conversion contracts offered were less than competitive with other company offerings.

The Transactional Sale

Another avenue that multiline companies attempted to enter was the transactional sale. The companies would provide turnkey programs for personal lines CSRs to prospect for life sales. Since they were only attempting to sell term insurance, why not create a simple-to-follow script for CSRs when conducting auto or homeowner's business? Here again, Littell and McSpadden got it right in *Crossing the Line* when they said,

One might at first glance think that cross-selling L&H has to be pretty similar to cross-selling personal lines, but this is not the case. The subject matter of the two product lines also produces distinct psychological reactions in the customer. There is a big difference, emotionally, between considerations of one's death and contemplating the loss of a piece of property. Death, after all, seems to mean the loss of everything in the world. It is of ultimate significance to the person—all other loss pales in comparison. Ensuring that one's house can be repaired after a windstorm is sensible and conservative; dying, on the other hand, is an almost unimaginable act—difficult at best to talk about. The sales process for life insurance must then be quite a bit different than for P&C.[4]

> Although there are ways for agency CSRs to assist in the prospecting of life clients, it isn't an easy task. Every company, including Travelers, offered some kind of program. I've never seen one of them succeed.

This is a good time to equate or, at least, somehow relate the P/C CSR to a position at a bank or credit union. That position would be the teller. Quite often, the tellers are the people who have face-to-face relationships with the customers. Here again, their duties are transactional. So how do they play a vital part in the overall marketing plan of the institution? We'll discuss that later in the book.

THE RESULTS

When I joined the Travelers in late 1981, they were beginning to phase out their career agent program. At that time, the Fort Lauderdale office housed only two SRTs (sales representatives in training). Apparently, Travelers learned early on that training career agents was an expensive proposition. But they were not quite ready to give it up altogether just to modify the program. Their next program was called the AAP program. The AAP plan was more broad based and flexible. The agent's assistance plan was, in essence, an advance commission program. We would contractually provide up-front funding for an independent agent or to an agency to hire a financial services producer.

Every Monday morning, all production supervisors were required to meet with the marketing manager to review and discuss their activities of the previous week. These meetings were called weekly planning sessions.

Honestly, these sessions were sometimes difficult to endure. If the previous week was not favorable from a production point of view, these forty-five-minute sessions seemed to last for hours. Here are two paragraphs from a memorandum reminding the production supervisors of what was expected of them at the planning session:

The weekly activity and production report which reflects the activity for the prior week should include the planned activity for the week and reflect, in a brief fashion, on a daily basis with whom, where, when, and for what reason the activity occurred. The actual activity for the prior week should reflect weighted premium results and occurrences that are worthy of mentioning. The reverse side of the prior week's activity should reflect any activity such as LP's, LB's, Experienced AAP's, accompanied by the actual commission results and compensation as outlined in the production analysis.

The rear of the sheet should also include the number of individual sales calls for a Travelers agent, the joint sales calls for a Travelers agent, the number of agency visitations and personal sales solicitations. Under the comments section, your assigned weighted premium quota should be reflected, the pro-rata goal should also be included and the actual results should be reflected.

As you can see, a Travelers production supervisor had a busy week and was held accountable for the activities of his or her multiline agencies. Although these weekly sessions were sometimes grueling, we learned quickly how to get results. We learned to listen to our agents and understand their needs, their abilities, and their desires. We understood how to market to their clients, how to create customized programs for their agencies, and how to generate consistent sales!

CHAPTER 3

The Proof Is in the Pudding

According to Bartlett's *Familiar Quotations*, the phrase dates back to at least 1615 when Miguel de Cervantes published *Don Quixote*. In this classic novel, the phrase is stated as "The proof of the pudding is the eating."[5] The only way to judge the true value of something is to put it to use and measure the results.

So it was time for me to eat! It was September of 1984, and I had been successfully working with several multiline agencies throughout southern Florida. My production numbers were strong, but something was missing. I longed for the good old days of radio management. It wasn't really radio that I missed but the satisfaction I felt from the creative aspects of the business.

In the radio business, I was a program director. The program director, in simple terms, is responsible for everything you hear on the air. I was fortunate enough to be working in the industry during the transitional years of the mid '70s. They were the transitional years in that several new formats were emerging, and the creative juices were flowing. Many program directors would never have the opportunity to do what I did in just a few short years. Here's why.

After paying my dues at small stations in Pennsylvania and Massachusetts,

I was offered the opportunity to program a station in a medium-market city. Stations are classified into categories by their potential audiences. All radio people aspire to work in a major market, but few ever make it.

At that time, there was a new format appearing in major cities called "mellow." Mellow referred to the smooth sound of the songs being programmed. Mellow programming was touted as the '70s version of beautiful music. Beautiful music stations programmed the stuff our parents listened to like Mantovani, the Boston Pops, and similar artists. Mellow was to be a contemporary new format designed for flow and sound. So long as the sound was there, we programmed almost anything, regardless of its commercial appeal. It was considered bold and esoteric at the time.

This exciting new format was rapidly gaining audiences in cities like New York and Los Angeles. The New York station WKTU, Mellow Music FM 92, took the city by storm, catering to New York's beautiful people, hip young people, and the Big Apple's chief person or so their ad stated in *New York Magazine.* I guess the best way to describe this sound was "soft rock." This exciting new sound rapidly moved up the East Coast when WWYZ, or YZ for short, hit the Hartford market.

My employers at WMAS in Springfield, Massachusetts, were from New York and were impressed with the rapid popularity of WKTU. So I was called into a meeting with the station principals and asked to develop a mellow format for WMAS-FM. I was given eight weeks to design the format, program the music, and hire the on-air staff. Think of it like this: You're called into a meeting where you are being asked to create a format that has a certain sound or feel. You've got to translate words into a flowing musical format in your mind. Once you've done that, you must physically build it. I call that a creative challenge.

If you want to know the final result I built it, and it worked. The station was elevated from ninth to third in total audience in the Springfield market. Success was short lived when mellow faded quickly, only to be replaced by disco. Fortunately, I was out of radio when that happened!

I really didn't want to go back into radio, but I wanted to use my creativity to work in an agency. And I wanted to take what I had learned at the Travelers to another level of success.

I had been quite successful in a small personal lines agency as a production supervisor. The owner of the agency and I had spoken on several occasions about the possibility of making it a permanent relationship.

I decided to leave the Travelers in January of 1985 and join the SPL (Small Personal Lines) agency. The first thing we did was determine our business structure. We formed a corporation. I owned 49 percent; they owned 51 percent. Next, we created my compensation schedule, perhaps the most important part of the initial negotiations. They had no idea how to put a package together, and my Travelers training was also a bit short in that area. The AAP program was developed to assist an agency in recruiting a full-time financial services producer but didn't always work as well as planned. I decided to propose my own compensation solution.

COMPENSATION

At the Travelers, we were permitted to do some personal production. I had a small book of business and continued to service my list of clients. I agreed to put any renewals I received into the coffers of the new corporation. In turn, the SPL agency would provide the following compensation package for the first twelve months:

- Months one through three: 100 percent of agreed-upon salary
- Months four through twelve: 100 percent of submitted annualized commission, not to exceed the agreed-upon salary. Any excess will be banked for any month where the submitted annualized commission fell short of the agreed-upon salary.

Since I transferred all my renewals into the corporation, SPL's risk would be minimal, less than three months of salary. And the transfer of renewals provided something more, my financial participation. Although a small number, my commitment to this new business relationship was important.

It would be naïve to assume that the new corporation would immediately generate commission. By structuring the compensation package around submitted annualized commission, the principal of SPL would be providing an advance in months four through twelve, collateralized by written production. So, if something went wrong, SPL agency would be made whole within a period of twelve months.

Next, we were challenged to build an internal structure. The SPL agency had merged with another small personal lines agency in the previous year. Therefore, I was dealing with multiple producers.

So many agencies cannot create a workable structure for financial services production. Producers must all be on the same page. When you have P/C producers who want to write their own cases to receive more commission, your entire program is challenged. It is challenged for a few reasons: These rogue producers apparently feel they can generate as much or more commission with their clients as the financial services producer can generate. If they feel that way, then they probably don't trust your ability to work directly with their clients. Either way, you have a problem. I've seen so many financial services departments fall apart because of this lack of synergy.

At the SPL agency, we were fortunate enough to have all producers on the same page. Since I had worked with both agencies prior to the merger, I was a proven entity and had the full confidence of all producers. Nevertheless, we did allow the producers to write their own cases, although we made it clear that it was not our preferred method. Any agents who wrote their own cases would receive 40 percent commission. If the financial services department wrote the case, the agent would receive 30 percent commission. My expertise far exceeded the 10 percent difference in the schedules. The producers referred all cases to the financial services department.

The Marketing Plan

First of all, remember that we are going back to 1985. We were in our infancy regarding computers, did not have e-mail, and were just turning the corner with fax machines. Our printers were dot matrix and took forever to print a proposal.

Introduction and Announcement

The introduction and announcement letter was sent to all policyholders, both personal and commercial lines. The letter merely announced the addition of a center for financial services within the SPL agency. We touted our service relationship and our commitment to provide professional analysis of their personal and business financial needs.

All producers and CSRs were provided a copy of the letter and briefed on its significance. They were also instructed how to handle any queries.

RED CARPET INTRODUCTIONS

We didn't need any of the above to implement our most profitable action plan. We are in the life insurance business, and we are relationship oriented. We sell face to face, and we help our clients understand the human asset risks they face every day. Simply put, we disturb them. No clients ever bought life insurance policies from me unless they realized their mortal nature.

I asked each producer to provide a personal introduction to his or her most important clients. I asked the producer not to discuss any products with the client, just provide a brief introduction regarding our new service offerings. After the introduction, the producer asked the client to grant me a thirty-minute appointment.

If the client was a commercial insurance customer, we planned the introduction prior to the renewal date. This was done so the client could focus on my presentation and not be concerned with any renewal increases, etc.

Most P/C agents do not realize the influence they have with their clients. For example, as a production supervisor, I would make a compelling presentation, only to have the P/C client look to the agent for his or her confirmation. With the nod of a head, the sale was consummated. It was that simple!

The red carpet introduction action plan will always produce the best results. It's also a solid confirmation that everyone at the agency is on board with you.

VISUAL DISPLAYS AND TIMELY MAILERS

Prior to on-demand printing, insurance companies produced a plethora of printed marketing materials for their agency forces. The agency could order anything from complete estate planning guides to envelope-sized stuffers. Have you ever seen the little cardboard display saying, "We sell life insurance?" From marketing concepts to specific product materials, all were available to order in substantial quantities.

At the SPL agency, we purchased a display rack to hold various marketing materials from our key carriers. The rack was openly displayed in our lobby area. When clients arrived for appointments, I would make sure they had sufficient time to peruse all the materials in the lobby prior to inviting them into my office. You'd be surprised how effective this simple idea can be!

An IRA stuffer in January is an example of a timely mailer. Any mail going out from the agency was stuffed with a concept or product piece. These pieces were provided free of charge from our companies and did not cost the agency any additional postage.

In addition, whenever we used a stuffer (almost every week), we notified all the producers of the stuffer content so they could bring it up when speaking with their clients.

SEMINARS

Financial planning was a very hot topic in 1985 as the major insurance companies made an attempt to compete with the more established wire houses. Travelers seemed to be in the forefront with cash management products like Capital T. In addition, they owned a money management firm and aggressively promoted their services to qualified investors.

As a registered representative of TESI (Travelers Equity Sales, Inc.), I was properly licensed to market all equity products offered by the broker/dealer.

We initially identified qualified clients in the agency and scheduled an evening seminar on private money management, sponsored by the SPL agency and the Massachusetts Company.

The seminar was well received and over the course of two years generated over three million in equity sales.

NEWSLETTER

Following our initial money management seminar, we introduced our quarterly newsletter. We addressed a myriad of topics every quarter, from the need for a personal umbrella policy to disability income. Most importantly, we stressed our recurring theme: one-stop shopping!

The SPL newsletter proved to be a powerful marketing tool. All agency clients received the newsletter. In many cases, it was passed on to other family members and generated substantial sales from referrals.

CLIENT SURVEYS

Once a year, all clients of the SPL agency would receive a survey, either personal lines or commercial lines. The introductory letter detailed our desire to better serve our clientele by providing the necessary services to meet their needs. We asked them to complete the survey and return it in the envelope provided. The return rate was approximately 20 percent.

EVENT FORMS

We previously discussed the role of the CSR or bank teller in the overall scheme of the marketing plan. Selling or promoting an intangible product is really above and beyond the transaction-oriented service representative's call of duty. Remember, all the major P/C companies had a CSR program of some kind or another. Regardless of their structure, they all failed.

At the SPL agency, we understood the true value of our CSRs. They were in direct contact with our agency clients on a regular basis. The question was how we could use their contact with clients to grow our financial services division.

The answer was simple: make our CSR program transactional. We created event forms. If any of the events listed on the form had taken place with the agency client, the CSR merely checked the appropriate box and turned the form in at the end of the day.

CSRs were rewarded for prudently completing the forms. They were not required to sell anything and were rewarded with gift cards and free lunches.

THE OCTOPUS

Look at each action plan as a tentacle. Each action plan could be evaluated over the course of the year. If a plan was successful, we determined how to expand it; if it was not successful, we considered an alternate plan. Overall, by having multiple action plans function simultaneously, we were successful.

QUANTIFIABLE RETURNS

Starting a new company is difficult enough, but proving your worth can be even more confusing. The first thing I did was build a spreadsheet on Lotus 1-2-3, the predecessor to Excel. Each application written was logged with all the details, including the annualized compensation. Remember the structure of my compensation package: everything was based on annualized commission. My goal was to write twenty or more cases per month. I really didn't care if I wrote a short-term hospital plan or a twenty-person group. Every case got counted. My yearly goal was to exceed 250 written cases.

At the beginning of each month, I would present a report to the other stockholders (51 percent) detailing written business and annualized commissions from the previous month. Although the cash flow was slow to increase, it was obvious from the production report that my draw was adequately collateralized. I sincerely believe that had I not presented my productivity so vividly, my new partners may have pulled the plug prematurely. I assured them, month after month, that all advances were covered by solid production. And they were!

The spreadsheet program also overtly demonstrated to the producers the results of their referrals and introductions. After the first year, the cash flow was beginning to catch up with the production. Then, we hit the mother lode. We were given the opportunity to compete for a six million investment account. As it turned out, we were given two million, two million went to a wire house, and the remaining two million was invested in real estate. After that, our insurance and investment business seemed to grow steadily.

Our results were impressive and proved that a properly structured financial services division could generate collateralized revenue in a reasonable time frame.

UNFORESEEN CIRCUMSTANCES

Although I thought I had everything planned perfectly, I neglected to consider some of the personal issues involved in any new business venture. As the 49 percent stockholder of SPL Financial Services, Inc., I was in the minority. I had, on several occasions, informed the 51 percent stockholder that it was not unreasonable to anticipate a solid profit within four years. I needed three solid years to build my division as we had projected.

Sometime before the end of the second year, I felt considerable pressure from the 51 percent side to share our early profitability. I was concerned because we were still building, and any draining of revenue to stockholders, other than the salaries provided for employees of SPL Financial Services (myself and one assistant), could put our business in financial jeopardy.

When I initially conducted my due diligence, I neglected to study the mix of business within the SPL agency. As stated in the name, SPL stands for small personal lines. Although the agency was beginning to make progress in marketing more commercial coverage, it was predominately a homeowners and auto agency. It was also very closely held, as were so many small agencies at that time.

Apparently, certain family members of the 51 percent shareholder wanted to realize revenue from SPL Financial Services. As the driving force at SPL Financial Services, I was opposed to sharing any revenue until we were on more solid financial ground. I can only assume that my collateralized draw was creating a family issue. They were the blood, and I was the water.

The reason I share this detailed history is to demonstrate how carefully all aspects of the marketing plan must be thought out and agreed upon. I have seen so many relationships fail because of inadequate planning. I thought I had it all covered only to realize there were some pieces missing. I learned a very important lesson at SPL.

CHAPTER 4

Beltway Bandits

I realized that I would have ongoing issues with certain employees of the SPL agency and decided to weigh my options. Before I had time to even consider other opportunities, I was contacted by the marketing manager of the Washington, DC, office of the Travelers. They needed help. Over the years, the low-hanging fruit was all annuity business, and the Washington office was a leader in annuity production and a loser in life insurance production. The recently hired marketing manager wanted to grow the life insurance business and asked me make a trip to the nation's capital to discuss his plans for growth. We were scheduled to fly into Dulles on a Friday morning and interview with the Travelers management that morning. I say "we" since my wife was also being interviewed by the commercial lines department for an underwriting position. The day before our flight, the DC area got hit with a foot of snow. If you've ever been to the greater DC area in the winter, you know they can't handle snow. Although the area was paralyzed, we made the trip and met in a vacant Travelers office with the all lines manager, the commercial lines manager, and the financial services manager. All other employees were enjoying a snow day.

After negotiating two positions, we had positive feelings regarding relocation to northern Virginia. Travelers offered to pay all moving expenses, buy our house (if we could not sell privately), and put me up in temporary living facilities until all could be finalized. That's in addition to paying all closing costs on both ends. It was an offer we could not refuse!

As we boarded the plane to return to Fort Lauderdale on Sunday afternoon, the captain announced that we would be deiced prior to taking off. A few minutes later, we were in the air in the midst of another snow storm. Shortly after takeoff, the captain informed us that we were the last plane to take off and that Dulles was now closed. He then announced that there were sunny skies in Fort Lauderdale with a temperature of seventy-five degrees. All aboard cheered, except us! What were we getting into?

THE EXIT

It was difficult to exit the SPL agency. After all, it was really a work of love, and I would miss most of the people I worked with. I offered to help find a suitable replacement since we had a very functional division in just two short years. I also assured the 51 percent stockholder that all advances I received would be repaid according to our collateralized agreement, and they were. Unfortunately, the SPL agency chose not to take me up on my offer to help find a replacement. They terminated the division and went back to mediocre financial services production. Three years later, we settled out of court.

Life production in the Washington, DC, office of the Travelers ranked somewhere in the middle of the pack. Annuities were the easy sale in the mid '80s, particularly in an area of the country that was somewhat recession proof. There were so many government contracts floating around that almost every company tied to the feds had a qualified plan as well as other financial perks. Many of these companies were domiciled within or near the I-495 beltway, thus beltway bandits.

The production managers in the Washington office were very proficient in marketing annuity products, a result of the previous manager's preference. Travelers had just transitioned to a "monster manager" plan. The official title was all lines manager (ALM), one manager for all three disciplines. Imagine having one person in charge of commercial lines, personal lines, and financial services. Fortunately for me, the ALM in Washington was the former financial services manager. This one-size-fits-all plan was the brainchild of a senior-level executive and executed as his last major directive. It was short lived.

As part of the new system, Travelers had created a position called agency manager. The role of the agency manager was touted as the position of the future. Unfortunately for Travelers, the future was not as senior management had envisioned.

In fairness to Travelers management in the '80s, there is no doubt in this author's mind that they were the leader in cross marketing. So why not take it to the next level? The idea was simple: create a synergy between all three lines, leaving the competition in the cold.

The fate of the entire plan was in the hands of the ALM. Some of these managers were from commercial lines, some from personal lines, and some from financial services. So everyone had a different game plan. It was bizarre! Each understood management from his or her own perspective.

THE UNIT

I was given a unit of agencies scattered throughout northern Virginia, Maryland, and the District. Most of these agencies were Travelers multiline affiliates. None had a history of substantial life production. In fact, many of them were producing less than ten cases per year. Compared to southern Florida, however, there were substantially more Travelers agencies. In Fort Lauderdale, we were trained to go beyond the Travelers agency and contract any P/C agency that was open to our marketing plan. These new agencies were not very productive, but they were open to suggestion, and they did make me feel welcome.

As the new kid on the block, I was not looked on very favorably by my peers. Having previously worked with their new manager in Florida made me suspect. I was the outsider. This perceived attitude made me even more anxious and determined to succeed. I found solace in working longer and harder than the other managers. I visited my agency force on a regular basis, getting to know their staff and mix of business.

As I got to know my agencies, I realized that most of them had a strong desire to produce life business. I was pleasantly surprised when they were open to my ideas and marketing plans. They had never been offered the level of assistance I was bringing to the table.

I didn't take long to get the ball rolling, and the agencies assigned to my unit were writing life insurance. Well, more specifically, I was writing life insurance for them. The plan was working   they provided the red carpet introductions, and I wrote the applications. Having been successful in an agency in Florida had created the credibility I needed to enjoy a fast start. I could share my real life experiences while my competitors had less to work with.

Unit life sales increased steadily throughout year one in Washington, and my relationship with the multiline agencies had solidified. It appeared that several of the agencies were experiencing a generational shift. The agency principals were preparing to turn over the management and sales duties to their children. I saw this transitional period as a period of opportunity.

Early in the first quarter of year two, I was contacted by the principal of one of my multiline agencies and asked to meet him for lunch. When I arrived, the agency principal and his son were waiting for me. He (the dad) didn't seem very happy. The agency had been very loyal to me in the short time I'd been in the Washington field office and had made a commitment to growing their life business.

It turns out that a life career shop had been soliciting the son to join their company as an agent in training. They had apparently done a great job in convincing the young man that their program would make him quite successful. He was ready to sign on the bottom line. As a last-minute request, his father asked him to consult with me regarding this career shift. My life was about to change forever!

SOAP

During the course of the luncheon, I had an opportunity to view the career company's training manual and to learn more about the promises and commitments they had made to the young man. It was evident to me that the career company understood the potential value of contracting the son of a multiline agency owner.

Having been trained by two career companies, I also knew the young man was, in fact, being offered an opportunity! I had worked very hard to develop this agency and certainly didn't want to lose their production. On the other hand, I had no formal program to offer them. How could I compete with the *Green Book Company*? Yes, the training manual was green. You might guess the company name (assuming you were in the business in 1988).

The answer seemed obvious, but did I really want to go that far? The answer was a definitive *yes*! So, right then and there, in a Mexican restaurant in Woodbridge, Virginia, I committed to teaching a formal program to market financial services in a closely held property/casualty agency.

I decided to offer the program, consisting of twelve weekly three-hour sessions. The program was available to any agency in my unit that had second-generation producers or a newly formed financial services department. Four agencies signed on immediately, all consisting of sons of agency principals (SOAP). One additional agency signed up that had recently formed a financial services department and hired a former career agent to run it.

THE PROGRAM

In order to accurately determine the success of the SOAP program, I decided to do the following: Each session would be videotaped. Each session would consist of four distinct parts. Production goals would be established for each student and monitored weekly. All materials including sales concepts, product illustrations, and sales systems would be documented and saved.

It was my intent to someday expand the offering of this program to other agencies on a larger scale. Here we are in 2010, twenty-one years after that Mexican luncheon, and the program is as vital today as it was in 1989. Willie Nelson expressed it so aptly in his song, "Funny How Time Slips Away."

CHAPTER 5

Effective Financial Services Marketing in a Multiline Agency

OVERVIEW

The course was intended to be a hands-on program of effective marketing through product knowledge, personal communication, advertising, sales expertise, needs development, and strategic business planning.

Sessions were held weekly and consisted of four basic parts:

1. **Monitoring**: a class discussion and evaluation of the previous week's sales results.
2. **Product Discussion**: an in-depth analysis of all financial services products.
3. **Marketing**: a practical understanding of how we get our products and services to our clients.
4. **Telemarketing:** direct client telephone contact to schedule appointments for the coming week.

Upon successful completion of the course, each student was equipped with the necessary skills to profitably manage a financial services department within a multiline agency. It is important to note that prior to developing the course, I received a written confirmation and commitment from all agency principals. All participants were required to attend every session and participate 100 percent in assigned activities. Here's a summary of each week's activities and discussions.

WEEK ONE

Week one started off with an upside down look at the entire course, starting with the expected results and how they were to be achieved. We then discussed our goal of explaining the inherent advantage each student had over the quintessential life insurance career agent. Next, we discussed the comprehensive nature of the program and what the future held in store upon successful completion of the course.

MONITORING

Since it was the first week, there were no production results to discuss. It was an excellent time to discuss each agent's previous financial services activity. We discussed their histories in financial services marketing and discussed how and where improvements could be made.

Then, we designed each agent's sales goals for the following twelve months, taking into consideration total hours devoted each week to financial services. We also further defined each agent's goals in terms of total written weekly premium. All of the agents set goals of how many appointments they wanted to schedule weekly, how many sales they wanted to make weekly, and the average commission they wanted to generate from each sale.

PRODUCT DISCUSSION

On week one, we started with a very basic discussion of life insurance. I discussed the evolution of life insurance and how each and every product consists of but three components: mortality, interest, and expenses.

MARKETING

From this point on, I'd like to present my notes as initially written and presented to the students. You should be able to follow the weekly progression as each student advances his or her skill levels in sales and marketing.

We'll start with the marketing notes from week one.

Marketing   Initiate a group discussion on the definition of marketing.

Marketing: the effective exposure of a product or service in the desired demographic or any other targeted area. Marketing involves everything from advertising, packaging, sales service, and research and development.

What skills does a person need to market successfully?

A thorough understanding of what it is he or she is marketing, who needs it and why, and whether enough people need it to make it profitable to the company. He or she must also know how to cost effectively get the product or service to the consumer, how to stay ahead of the competition, when to change and evolve the product or service, etc.

Are these skills learned or innate?

Although some people may be more innately gifted with marketing skills (common sense) than others, I strongly feel that marketing skills can be learned through a series of systematic logical steps.

What is the most important factor in the success or failure of a business today?

Marketing is the most important factor.

Conclusion

Strongly stress that marketing skills are learned skills, and they are learned through a systematic and simple approach that anyone who has the desire to achieve success can learn. The sky is the limit once proper marketing skills have been learned.

Marketing in Your Agency

Multiline Marketing (Advantages and Disadvantages)

Advantages:
1.   Client base
2.   Relationship already developed
3.   Natural progression of risk assessment

Disadvantages:

1. Lack of knowledge
2. Lack of confidence
3. Fear of destroying relationship
4. Image of life salesperson

The first two disadvantages are valid but can be easily overcome with proper training. The third and fourth disadvantages are not valid and are created in the minds of the agent, not the client.

Property/Casualty Marketing vs. Financial Services Marketing

Explain the cliff theory: When a property/casualty agent makes his or her first sale, it's usually by providing better coverage for the customers at a rate below their current premiums. Over the years, the agent develops a strong service relationship with the clients. Understanding this relationship is the key to successful cross marketing. The life sale should be based on a disciplined marketing strategy of value-added service. Marketing financial services is exactly that: marketing services, not products. Since the agency already has a client base developed by successful servicing, the financial services progression is extremely natural, assuming it's implemented properly.

Credibility is worthiness of belief. The agent bridges the gap between property/casualty and financial services by explaining the similarities of property risks and another kind of risk, human asset risk.

Creative Logic

This, simply put, is the development of the proper thought patterns to create marketing ideas and to understand how marketing can be applied to almost every situation. The student must have a strong desire to succeed and to realize that a systematic understanding of marketing is the most effective way to succeed.

Creative logic may be one of the most important components of the course. It must be constantly imprinted into the minds of the students so they can develop their own creative logic skill levels. Create assignments to help achieve these skills. Reinforce to each student that he or she has the ability to be a creative marketer.

Championship Team Theory

Ask the students if any of them were ever members of championship teams. If so, ask them if they understand exactly what happens when a team is elevated to championship status.

First of all, a championship team plays as a team, creating a synergy that is nonexistent in their competition. But more importantly, every player plays at the level of their most talented player, creating a winning combination. Think of it this way: have you ever been in a zone? Everything just seems to go the right way. It's not an accident or pure luck! Our minds can help us achieve lofty goals, if only we believe.

What is a sale?

It is the elimination of all objections.

Are marketing and sales synonymous?

No, the sale is only part of the entire marketing experience. Don't give students the correct answer until you have discussed the next question.

Why or why not?

Facilitate a group discussion.

Who is a salesperson?

Stress here that everyone is a salesperson. The world revolves around sales. Give the students everyday examples of the art of persuasion and how things they do on a daily basis can help them with the insurance sales process.

TELEMARKETING

Talk about diving in head first! The first week of telemarketing was critical. Prior to starting the course, I was divided as to when I should actually put each student on the phone in a real life situation. If I did a good job in explaining the purpose of the call and the progression of the call (creative logic), I could instill a high level of confidence in the students right out of the box in week one.

On the other hand, if the plan didn't go as well as anticipated, my own credibility might become suspect. I decided to take the chance and put them on the phones the first week. Here's how I set the stage.

Each student would make two calls, one cold call from the local telephone book using the script from the *Green Book Company*, and one from a list of personal lines clients from their respective agencies.

I asked each agency principal to send me a list of fifty personal lines clients prior to the class. During the calling session, I randomly selected a name from the phone book. Then, each student would call (on speakerphone), armed with the *Green Book Company* script. No one was successful. In fact, three of the five parties called hung up on my novice students within the first thirty seconds of the conversation. Ouch! I can't remember exactly how the script read, but one of the lines went something like this: "Wouldn't you agree that it is better to have money than to not have money?" That's as far as anyone got into the script before they were cut off. All five students looked pretty dejected. We took a brief break.

After the break, I unveiled another script. This script was much shorter and simpler compared to the *Green Book Company* dissertation. Before selecting any clients to call, I armed each student with one more weapon, a list of answers to the seven most common objections. I told them that if any of these objections were presented, just answer the objection followed by another request for the appointment. When asking for the appointment, give the client the option of two different days and times.

Four of the five students successfully completed their assignment. They had scheduled appointments with agency clients for the following week. Incidentally, the unsuccessful fifth student had a different background than the other four. He had just joined a property/casualty agency, having been trained in a career shop. He was not the son of the agency principal and had arrived at the class with a bit of a chip on his shoulder. It was obvious that he thought he had more skills than the other students in the class. Unfortunately, he could not differentiate between product knowledge and sales skills. He deviated from the script within the first ten seconds of the conversation and created his own answers to the objections. He failed, not only in attempting to schedule an appointment, but overall. He dropped out of the class in week seven and left the agency shortly thereafter.

I wished the result had been better for him, but his obvious failure served to reinforce the bond I had developed with the other students. I'm sure 80 percent of them slept well that night.

WEEK TWO

We started off week two with a review of our established goals, followed by the results of the previous week's activities. We discussed the ease of securing an appointment with an agency client and the fact that prospecting would not be a problem, so long as we stayed the course. The big question was this: What do we do after securing the appointment?

Each student had very basic product and sales skills. So, every week, I devoted a substantial part of the class to product training: life insurance, annuities, major medical, disability, and long-term care insurance.

In addition, they needed a sales system. I had been a strong advocate of Tom Wolfe's capital needs analysis (CNA) from my early days in the business. In fact, I had progressed from CNA to financial needs analysis I (FNA I), a more comprehensive analysis than CNA. In 1988, we had financial needs analysis II (FNA II), consisting of client presentation materials and in-depth training tapes and visuals for the students. Almost all career companies used Tom Wolfe's materials to train their agents. Everything was addressed, from securing the appointment to delivery of the policies.

The students were required to use FNA II for all their appointments. In the first several weeks, ninety minutes of our three-hour session was devoted to FNA training.

In week two telemarketing, each student was asked, once again, to make a cold call from the phone book using the *Green Book Company* script. The results were very similar to those of the previous week. The purpose of the cold call was to solidify in their minds the absolute value of their agency relationship with their clients. No more cold calls, no more prospecting woes.

AND SO IT GOES

Without subjecting you to the minute details of each week's session, I will provide a review of the four main components of the course. The purpose of the review is to analyze exactly how and why these components, individually and collectively, contributed to the overall success of the course.

MONITORING

Every week, we would initiate our session with a discussion of our previous week's activities. We would discuss our goals for the week and our results for the week. The group would discuss what went right and what went wrong. I would act as the moderator of the discussion, but only actively participate when asked or to identify an obvious issue.

The group drew its strength from each other. They learned from each other's mistakes and developed a common bond. As the course progressed, the students' overall participation increased substantially. They looked forward to sharing their successes among themselves as well as commiserating with each other.

We reviewed their business plans, their commitment to monitor their action plans and make necessary changes, and their commitment to success.

WHY WAS MONITORING SUCCESSFUL?

Monitoring was successful because each student designed his or her own goals. He or she determined exactly how many hours per week would be devoted to financial services marketing, how many appointments he or she would schedule, how many sales he or she would make, and the average premium generated per sale.

It was their program, not mine. I was merely their mentor, the person they turned to when they needed guidance and understanding. I was the record keeper, providing visual evidence of their results. And the results were quite impressive, as you will see.

PRODUCT DISCUSSION

We started at the very beginning. We discussed the three components of any life insurance product. Then, I started with ART and progressed all the way to variable life. I discussed products that they never sold, like participating whole life. But most of all, I taught them to understand the products and to be objective. They learned about mortality tables and reserves. They learned the good and the bad points of universal life, interest sensitive whole life, whole life (par and non-par), variable life, and survivorship life. Overall, they learned about life insurance and that every product has a place.

We followed the same procedure with annuities, disability income insurance, major medical, and long-term care. We read policies, both new and old.

We discussed contractual provisions, the unilateral nature of insurance contracts, non-forfeiture provisions, and on and on.

I wanted the students to quickly develop a proficiency in product construction. If they knew enough about the history and development of insurance products, they would not be hesitant to approach clients of the agency. They were also taught that no one person has all the answers. If they encountered difficult situations, their backup teams were ready to help.

But product knowledge is only the first part of the overall success of the product discussion module.

Each week, following the basic presentation of a product, I would present a creative use of the product. From a formal annuity marketing program to the flexible uses of universal life, the students were subjected to thought-provoking ways to present their portfolios. For example

Creative Universal Life Applications

Week Four

- Have a student explain how a universal life policy works
- Show creative flexibility of UL ($0 CV vs. endowment)
- Ask students for creative UL situations

Week Five

- Discuss term riders, cost of living and other riders, and their uses

Week Six

- Discuss how to compare universal life contracts   look beyond the numbers
- Discuss other company's products and the differences in structure
- Discuss loading (front, middle, etc.)
- Discuss mortality and assumptions used in current tables
- Stress value-added and creative ways to pay premiums

My ultimate goal was simple   provide each student with a workable understanding of the product and its practical application in the field. And do it in twelve weeks.

MARKETING

From a marketing perspective, I wanted the students to develop their own selling system utilizing the concepts of the cliff theory, the wedge, creative logic, and the championship team theory. Each week, they enhanced their role-playing FNA skills, including the appropriate risk analysis and appropriate subsequent presentation.

I wanted them to learn to be creative and think on their own with all the rote skills of the best selling systems, customized to their unique personalities.

Every week, I discussed the progress of each student with their respective agency principals. We discussed their progress in sales development as well as their productivity and progress as measured by their individual business plans. The students knew they had three people to answer to: themselves, their agency principals, and lastly, me.

The fact that they scheduled their appointments for the week each Monday night created a sense of team spirit.

OBJECTIVES

Remember, each agent set goals of how many appointments they wanted to schedule weekly, how many sales they wanted to make weekly, and the average commission they wanted to generate from each sale. Here are the objectives and results over a fifteen-week period:

GOALS

Average number of appointments per week: 3.5

Average Sales per week: 1.5

Average commission per sale: $500

RESULTS

Number of appointments per week: 3.4

Sales per week: 1.53

Commission per sale: $650

From the final tally, the students exceeded their established commission goal by $150 per sale or 130 percent of the objective. That's an annual run rate of nearly $45,000. It is noteworthy to remember that the students were property casualty agents, focusing only part time on financial services. Increasing their revenue by $45,000 would be considered a huge success for a neophyte career agent, let alone a property casualty agent working part time!

Unfortunately, I never had the opportunity to take the program to the next level. I had promised my wife that we would be returning to Florida within three years. So I started my search in late 1989 to make my pilgrimage back to the Sunshine State. I had thought that sometime between 1987 and 1990, a branch office management position would open up in either Tampa or Orlando. That didn't happen, so I was resigned to return in a lateral position to Fort Lauderdale.

After negotiating my move and new position, rumors were beginning to spread regarding another corporate reorganization. I soon realized that it was not a rumor but actually happening. All transfers had been put on hold, but no one contacted me.

I'd like to share with you a letter received by my supervisor, Thomas Holland, from one of the agency principals in December 1989. The entire program was a huge success and really gave me a tremendous feeling of satisfaction. Having left the SPL agency without reaching our potential was difficult. Teaching these young students to achieve success in such a short period of time didn't make up for unfinished business at SPL but certainly cemented the basic premise behind our cross-marketing program.

Here's the letter:

> *Now that 1989 is winding down, it's time to reflect on past events and thank specific people who have contributed to the success of our agency.*

The person who is at the top of the list is Marlin Bollinger. Under your able supervision, he developed an outstanding program for sons of agency principals (SOAPS!). I received a double benefit since both of my sons attended his classes. Chuck was fortunate enough to attend from the beginning, although Donald was not licensed until midway through. The sales training along with the product knowledge that they received was exceptional. Even if I could have found similar instruction in the area, the costs would probably have been prohibitive. Donald, who sold copiers for four years and thereby received extensive sales training, was greatly impressed. The classes transformed Chuck into a superior sales person. As you know all of this was done in the evening after hours.

How has Travelers benefitted? They are receiving a steady flow of LHFS applications and along with them a steady stream of loyalty. Both sons are in the twenties, so your company will be enjoying the fruits of Marlin's labor long into the future. I'm so impressed and grateful for this splendid training that I would like to invite you and Marlin and your spouses to be my guests at dinner on December 15th. Of course, the "boys" and their companions will be there along with my wife. This will be a "Marlin Bollinger Appreciation Night!" I'll be in touch with you as to time and place. Once again, thank you from a very appreciative, long time (26 years) Traveler's agent.

Sincerely,

Charles B. Gibson, Sr. CLU, ChFC, MFS

CHAPTER 6

I-95 South

Although most transfers had been stopped, my return to Florida proceeded without interruption. I was scheduled to report to the Fort Lauderdale field office on April 1, three years to the day since I had left the SPL agency. Upon reporting to the all lines manager, I was told to go home, take my time moving in, and return in two weeks. At that point, I realized that the reorganization was in progress, and my transfer had not been stopped for a reason. What that reason was, I didn't yet know and apparently would not know for two weeks!

CENTERSOURCE

While in the Washington, DC, office, I was recruited to work with the home office marketing department in the development of a comprehensive program titled CenterSource. As we developed the program, I was regularly reminded that this program didn't have to be successful; it was a pilot. I found it strange that a company would put forth the physical and financial resources unless they intended the pilot to be successful. Here's the CenterSource introduction:

Studies and surveys indicate that most agency owners agree (today more than ever before) that it is vital to

1. Provide total customer support,

2. Retain client base and reduce P/C competition,
3. Improve pre-tax profit margins,
4. Raise the average revenue per producer,
5. Attract new customers, and
6. Create positive agency image and community presence.

The same studies show that one proven way of achieving these results is through selling a full array of financial services products to existing clients as well as to new clients.

Many agency owners tell us that they need help in establishing financial services expertise in their agencies. And this is why CenterSource has been created.

The CenterSource objective is to assist selected high potential agencies in establishing their own financial services facilities through the use of a focused package of Travelers resources and discipline supported by qualified Travelers staff.

CenterSource is a functional arrangement of existing home office support services and marketing resources that presents a roadmap to help an agency build its image in the community as being a source for financial services, to establish meaningful financial services goals, and to build a logical sequence of disciplined marketing activities to achieve these goals.

The program consisted of five basic segments:
1. Agency selection and readiness assessment,
2. Customer service survey,
3. Agency transition and marketing plan development,
4. Program implementation, and
5. Monitoring.

CenterSource never evolved beyond the planning stage as the agency marketing group was dissolved with the reorganization of 1990.

RETURN IN TWO WEEKS

When I returned to the Fort Lauderdale office two weeks into April, I was informed of the dissolution of the AMG and introduced to my new regional director. As it turned out, I was replacing the Fort Lauderdale marketing manager. He was, in turn, being relocated to Miami. The all lines manager was gone and the company was returning to vertical monoline management.

The company's financial services division would be divided into twenty-five regions, two of which would be in Florida. The reorganization of 1990 was significant for the Travelers. It was their initial entry into independent distribution beyond the narrow property/casualty channel.

Although only a few of us knew of CenterSource, the program was not entirely forgotten. After the reorganization, two new programs were introduced into our marketing scheme: Add-A-Pro and the ABCs of Generating Leads. Both programs were an offshoot of CenterSource.

Add-A-Pro was a premium financing program offered to qualified property/casualty agencies. The Travelers would provide the initial funding to hire the producer. Debt reduction and interest rate reduction could be achieved as production increased.

The ABCs of Generating Leads was designed to offer action plans for the agencies to increase financial services production. The process was based on the fact that approximately one in ten agency clients will purchase some form of financial services product in any given twelve-month period. The lead generation system was a process designed to increase the number of leads for Travelers financial services products from an agency's existing book of property/casualty business.

Prior to the evolutionary '80s, most insurance companies would release their products in series. Life insurance products were relatively static in the 1950s through the 1970s. There was term insurance and permanent whole life insurance. Of course, there were choices among the two basic forms, but overall, things remained fairly predictable. Insurance policies are contracts. Contracts have guarantees, guaranteed mortality, interest, and expenses.

With the advent of universal life, insurance companies were given substantially more latitude to develop products with more flexibility. There were the contractual guarantees but also current assumption interest rates and current mortality projections. Companies could complete with each other based upon their determined terms. Any attempt to compare one company's universal life policy with that of another company was extremely difficult, if not impossible! The only factors that could be compared were the guarantees. With high current interest rates, almost all agents were selling the current assumptions.

Travelers realized in the early '90s that they could not survive unless they entered independent distribution. By entering a new distribution channel, it was necessary to develop products on a regular and consistent basis in order to compete in the marketplace. A company could no longer sit back while developing a complete series of products to be introduced simultaneously.

EVOLUTION

The Travelers financial services department was eventually separated from the property/casualty departments. Travelers Life and Annuity became one of the top brokerage life insurance companies in the country. The twenty-five regions were eventually reduced, following several more reorganizations, to just four. In early 2005, Metlife announced their purchase of Travelers Life and Annuity for 11.5 billion dollars. Citigroup would spinoff Travelers and their international insurance businesses for one to three billion dollars in Metlife stock and the remainder in cash. The final sales price was $11.8 billion. Metlife became the largest seller of US life insurance overnight.

LOOKING BACK

Those of us who devoted years of our insurance careers to the development and evolution of the Travelers life department have fond memories of our achievements and shortcomings. We will never forget the satisfaction we received by working with all our friends at Travelers property/casualty agencies. There is no doubt that Travelers was always on the cutting edge in multiline marketing, from their cross-selling programs to their premature entry into the financial planning arena. Travelers aggressively marketed total financial planning opportunities in the mid '80s when other companies were only in the initial stages. Unfortunately, it appeared to be too much, too soon, and too expensive to maintain. All P/C agencies were offered a program called Capital T, an agency cash management program. Once comfortable with the product, agencies were afforded the opportunity to market Capital T to their clients. In addition to banking and investment services, Travelers also offered competitive mortgage programs through TMS, Travelers mortgage services. They were also one of the first companies to mass market personal computers to their agency force through another company they owned.

For the more advanced agencies, they offered mentoring in developing their own brokers/dealers. They owned the Massachusetts Company, a private money management firm, and marketed annuities through a subsidiary, Keystone Provident Life Insurance Company.

All in all, it was a great run, and those of us who were privileged enough to be there gained a wealth of knowledge!

CHAPTER 7

Hindsight

Fortunately, past performance is no guarantee of future results. That may be the case when it comes to investing, but may not hold true when it comes to cross marketing. If your agency didn't take definitive action to offer financial services in the past, your results were probably quite poor. If you don't take definitive action to market financial services in today's environment, I can almost guarantee your future results.

Peter Drucker once said, "It is far more important to do the right things than to do things right."[6] How often have you hesitated to expand your agency's financial services offerings, simply because you were not sure what to do or how to do it? Or you thought the expense would not justify the result. As I said earlier, those of us on the financial services side must assume much of the responsibility for not offering you simple and effective turnkey programs, and more importantly, for not communicating to you the programs we have offered.

In the July 1978 issue of the *Journal of Marketing*, Harvard Associate Professor of Business Administration Derek Abell wrote an article that is as timely today as it was some thirty-two years ago. He wrote an article titled "Strategic Windows: The Time to Invest in a Product or Market Is When a Strategic Window Is Open."[7] Here are some excerpts from the article:

STRATEGIC MARKET PLANNING involves the management of any business unit in the dual tasks of *anticipating* and *responding* to changes which affect the marketplace for their products. Anticipation of change and its impact can be substantially improved if an organizing framework can be used to identify sources and directions of change in a systematic fashion. Appropriate responses to change require a clear understanding of the alternative strategic options available to management as a market evolves and change takes place. ...

The term "strategic window" is used here to focus attention on the fact that there are only limited periods during which the "fit" between the key requirements of a market and the particular competencies of a firm competing in that market is at an optimum. Investment in a product line or market area should be timed to coincide with periods in which such a strategic window is open. ...

Among the most frequent questions which management has to deal with in this respect are: ...

• Should expenditure of funds of plant and equipment or marketing to support existing product lines be expanded, continued at historical levels, or diminished?
• When should a decision be made to quit and throw in the towel for an unprofitable product line or business area?

Resource allocation decisions of this nature all require a careful assessment of the future evolution of the market involved and an accurate appraisal of the firm's capability to successfully meet key marketing requirements. The strategic market concept encourages the analysis of these questions in a dynamic rather than a static framework, and forces marketing planners to be as specific as they can about these future patterns of market evolution and the firm's capacity to adapt to them. ...

Of key interest, however, is the question not only of where the firm is today but of how well equipped it is to deal with *tomorrow*. Such a *dynamic* analysis may foretell non-incremental changes in the market which work to disqualify market leaders, provide opportunities for currently low share competitors, and sometimes even usher in a completely new cast of competitors into the marketplace. ...

Frequently, as markets evolve, the fundamental definition of the market changes in ways which increasingly disqualify some competitors while providing opportunities for others. The trend towards marketing "systems" of products as opposed to individual pieces of equipment provides many examples of this phenomenon. ...

The "resource requirements" for success in a business—whether these be financial requirements, marketing requirements, engineering requirements, or whatever—may change radically with market evolution ... they appear to suggest that, by contrast, the firm's resources and key competencies often cannot be so easily adjusted. The result is a *predictable* change in the fit of the firm to its market—leading to defined periods during which a "strategic window" exists and can be exploited.

The "strategic window" concept can be useful to incumbent competitors as well as to would-be entrants into a market. For the former, it provides a way of relating future strategic moves to market evolution and of assessing how resources should be allocated to existing activities. For the latter, it provides a framework for diversification and growth. ...

All too frequently, however, because the "strategic window" phenomenon is not clearly recognized, these strategic choices are not clearly articulated. Instead, "old" approaches are continued long after the market has changed with the result that market position is lost and financial losses pile up. Or, often only half-hearted attempts are made to assemble the new resources required to compete effectively; or management is simply deluded into believing that it can adapt itself to the new situation even where this is actually out of the question. ...

The "strategic window" concept suggests that fundamental changes are needed in marketing management practice, and in particular in strategic market planning activities. At the heart of these changes is the need to base marketing planning around predictions of future patterns of market evolution and to make assessments of the firm's capabilities to deal with change. ...

Entry and exit from markets is likely to occur with greater rapidity than is often the case today, as firms search for opportunities where their resources can be deployed with maximum effectiveness. Short of entry and exit, the allocation of funds to markets should be timed to coincide with the period when the fit between the firm and the market is at its optimum.

Whether the year is 1978 or 2011, the concept of marketing when a "strategic window" is open is as fresh today as it was when first discussed.

CHAPTER 8

What Do You Market?

If you take a cold, hard look at your agency, are you marketing products or services? Are you offering your valuable clients the necessary services to achieve maximum success and risk protection in their environment, or are you just selling insurance products?

As I constantly visit and interview property/casualty agencies, I am beginning to see a real separation in their overall philosophical approach to marketing. Many agencies appear to be transitioning with the environment by offering the services required by their clients. Others are still adhering to the old school patterns of just focusing on the products with which they have a comfort level.

Today's progressive agencies focus proactively on total risk management. Not only are they focused on financial services but also on human resources issues and loss analysis. Their risk management programs are really partnerships that focus on creating proactive loss prevention programs. Staying ahead of the curve in difficult economic times is even more important than those prosperous times when we take our business for granted.

Cross-marketing financial services are a vital part of the entire program of loss prevention. Here are some helpful hints to get started:

- Partner with a firm that is service oriented, not product driven.
- Partner with a firm that is qualified to work with wealthy families, business owners, and high-income earners.
- Partner with a firm that has a structured sales system.
- Partner with a firm that focuses on solutions.
- Partner with a firm that offers a consultative sales process.
- Partner with a firm that demonstrates the ability and desire to build a long-range sustainable business.
- Partner with a firm that you trust.
- Partner with a firm that can offer you a total marketing experience.

Partnering with an outside company to provide professional services for your best clients requires proper due diligence. After all, these are your best clients, and you want to make sure they are provided the most comprehensive and professional services available. After garnering all the necessary references and bios, thoroughly review their consultative sales system to make sure their solutions-based marketing is a fit for your agency.

Next, enter into a mutually agreeable contract, detailing the responsibilities of all parties. Make sure that you are the servicing agent and that your agreement contains specific non-piracy clauses. All commissionable premium splits should be spelled out (see appendix).

Some agencies struggle with a fifty-fifty commission split. And, honestly, some outside firms also struggle with an equal split. Here's how I suggest you look at it. The outside marketing firm is providing a service that you are not capable of providing within your current agency structure. You are providing qualified prospects that the outside marketing firm needs to exist. Neither party has true value without the other. If you are committed to the program, and the outside firm can deliver the promised services, there will be sufficient profit for all parties involved.

CHAPTER 9

The Plan

Although we have discussed partnering with another firm or individual, it is important to discuss your agency's overall business plan. We are assuming that the agency does have an up-to-date business plan. If so, it will be necessary to build the marketing of financial services into the present plan in a functional and practical manner.

In chapter 3, we discussed a workable financial services marketing plan. Of course, every agency is a bit different from the next, although generically, most parts of the action plans in chapter 3 should work.

Initially, though, it is important to make sure your agency has a strong P/C business and marketing plan. I could write an entire book on business planning, but let's just make sure you have developed a successful P/C business plan prior to adding a financial services marketing plan. If you think your current plan is deficient, there are many websites that can provide a good outline to help you make any corrections you consider necessary. One example is www.125aday.com, a publishing company that offers multiple plans to help small businesses do more business.

FINANCIAL SERVICES MARKETING PLAN

For now, let's focus specifically on the financial services marketing plan.

There are essential elements to every plan, and each of these elements may be approached differently with similar results. Regardless of how you title these elements, they've all got to be in place to make your plan successful.

Successful cross marketing in the P/C world is really quite entrepreneurial. Michael E. Gerber, author of the E-Myth series of books, focuses on how moving from working in your business to on your business can be the difference between success and failure.[8] Mr. Gerber feels that a successful agency principal must wear three hats: technician, manager, and entrepreneur. He feels the entrepreneurial role within every insurance individual is the most important.

Now, let's focus on the system. Although germane to both P/C and financial services marketing, we'll concentrate on the financial services part here. To be successful in the marketing of life, annuity, and health products, you must have three systems in place: a lead generation system, a lead conversion system, and a client fulfillment system. Mr. Gerber refers to these three systems as your "core operating system" (COS). Your COS is your franchise and differentiates your franchise from everybody else's franchise.

We all know and can identify a successful franchise. Turning your COS into a successful turnkey system will set your franchise far apart from the competition.

Building your unique operating system will not be easy. On the other hand, it's not rocket science either. Mr. Gerber's approach to building your system is not one of time, but of desire. If you have the desire, you will make the time.

How many times have you been approached to develop a workable financial services marketing plan? And how many of those times did you use the excuse of being too busy or telling the other person that he or she didn't understand your business or your problem? Maybe he or she does understand your problem, and you don't.

A simple and workable financial services marketing plan can be divided into five areas.

OBJECTIVE

Here you state your ultimate objective. For example, the objective of the ABC Agency is to devise a workable multiline financial services marketing plan that will generate a minimum of (state your premium goals) from sales made to clients (commercial and personal) of the agency.

PURPOSE

Quite simply, the purpose should be to substantially increase the agency's financial services production.

PHILOSOPHIES

- You are the most important service your client buys.
- You provide the only service that can prevent financial trauma.
- Your customer is asking you to be the one-stop shopping service for all their insurance needs.

STRATEGIES

- Increase the agency's client awareness of the agency's financial services capabilities.
- Develop and implement a system of need selling to commercial lines clients of the agency.
- Develop and implement a system of cross selling financial services to personal lines clients of the agency.

ACTIVITIES

For each strategy adopted by the agency, activities or action plans must be developed that define the plans and programs to implement the strategy. For example, let's look at the first strategy.

Increase the agency's client awareness of the agency's financial services capabilities:

Need selling direct communication (e-mail, snail mail, or both) to commercial and personal lines clients,

Telephone follow up,

Account annual review (commercial and personal),

Human asset needs presentation to commercial clients.

These are a few examples of the backup action plans to support your agency's strategic goals. If you'd like a quick summary of the advantages of developing a financial services marketing plan, here are six great reasons to get started today:

1. Insulate your clients from the competition whose relationship with your clients may be, or could be, as strong as yours. Forcing your clients to go elsewhere for these services is placing them on proverbial silver plates for your competition. It is an accepted fact that the more business you have with the client, the less likely you are to lose the account.
2. Your clients will perceive you as providing a higher degree of professionalism and a more comprehensive service for them.
3. Profitability from these additional services could be equal to the profitability of your P/C operation, with much lower overhead.
4. Stabilize your agency as these additional services are not subject to the volatility that has been a historical problem in the P/C arena.
5. Increase the value of the agency and improve retention.
6. By improving the profitability and stability of the agency, you will be in a better position to buy additional agencies or alternatively increase the value of your agency, should you desire to sell or merge with another agency.

VPs AND USPs

I addition to all the activities and planning elements discussed so far, I suggest you consider adding two other very important propositions: a value proposition (VP) and a unique selling proposition (USP).

Understanding these two propositions will define your franchise value. They should be well thought out but short (one sentence for your VP and just a phrase for your USP). I'll go into more detail in the next chapter when we analyze the world of BGAs. Here is the Bollinger Group value proposition and unique selling proposition.

Value Proposition

Distribution source of competitive products and innovative marketing/ underwriting solutions to independent agents

Unique Selling Proposition

Better relationships start here!

CHAPTER 10

Brokerage General Agencies

YESTERDAY, TODAY, AND TOMORROW

A t the Bollinger Group, our clients are independent life, health, annuity, financial planning, and property/casualty agents and agencies throughout the United States. Our primary service is that of an intermediary, distributing financial services products for approximately thirty companies. If that was all we were, we would line up next to several hundred other brokerage general agencies.

Years ago, there were far fewer brokerage agencies. Each of these agencies represented only a few companies and had a regional presence and autonomy. In addition, there were insurance companies that specialized in substandard underwriting. Companies like US Financial, Fidelity Bankers, United of Omaha, and Empire General solicited impaired risks through their designated agencies. The primary purpose of these agencies was to secure the most favorable underwriting offers from the companies they represented. Many of the mainstream companies distributed their portfolios of products through career agents or directly to agents via personal producing general agent contracts. Brokerage agencies existed to write the cases the primary companies did not want. There were far fewer independent agents in those days, thus the bulk of brokerage sales were generated by career agents.

As the brokerage marketplace began to morph, so did the BGA world. Companies began to distribute their portfolios through the PPGA channel, the BGA channel, or both. In addition, BGAs slowly began to add more companies to their distribution lists. Companies with career agents were strapped to make a profit, because of their overly subsidized programs and revolving doors. Perhaps there was a better path to profitability with BGA distribution.

The Camel's Back

On Friday, March 21, 1980, President Jimmy Carter addressed TV cameras from the White House to announce yet another anti-inflation program. But, probably more importantly, he attempted to calm a national alarm that was bordering on panic. Interest rates and inflation had topped 18 percent. Americans were unsure and uncertain about the future of their country. The life insurance industry was also a very unsure and ruffled business.

Our products were relatively easy to understand. We sold whole life policies, participating (dividend paying) and non-participating. We sold term insurance, level, and decreasing. And we had just begun to sell a hybrid whole life/term product termed "economatic." These economatic-type products were approximately 70 percent whole life and 30 percent term insurance. As the respective company declared a dividend (overcharge of premium) to buy paid-up additional insurance, the term provision was reduced by the amount of additional insurance purchased by the dividend. Assuming the nonguaranteed dividend scale held up, a client could purchase whole life coverage for less than previously available. These whole life and economatic-type policies had a cash value that increased over the years and could either by surrendered for cash or borrowed against the collateralized cash value at a guaranteed rate of 5 or 6 percent.

The cash values of whole life insurance had previously only been invaded for emergency or educational purposes. And many of these policies were cash rich!

A degree in mathematics was not required to figure out that borrowing from your life insurance policy at 6 percent and reinvesting in a money market account at 18 percent, with minimal risk, would create a respectable profit, even after taxes! Well, you get the picture. It didn't take long for consumers to make a run on the insurance companies.

With their capital rapidly depleting, their career agents overly subsidized, and their portfolios of whole life products obsolete, life insurance companies realized that they had to make changes.

A SOLID STRUCTURE

Prior to the late 1970s, insurance products performed well throughout the years. All life insurance products consist of three parts: mortality, interest, and expenses. Whole life products were and are unilateral contracts; so long as the insured pays the premium on a timely basis, the insurance company is obligated to meet the contractual terms of the policy. In simple terms, the interest part of the trilogy is referred to as the reserve basis of the contract. After expenses and mortality charges have been levied, the remaining premium is credited with the reserve basis of the contract, creating a cash value account. The mortality charges are based on a uniform table called CSO. The commissioner's standard ordinary table of rates per thousand is used in whole life policies. The CSO table in existence in 1970 was from 1958. In fact, the table was not revised until 1980. Prior to the 1958 table, the 1941 table was used. The reserve basis on many old whole life contracts was as low as 2 or 3 percent.

WHEN E. F. HUTTON TALKS

If you're old enough to remember, you'll recall the old E. F. Hutton television commercials. The hook phrase was "When E. F. Hutton talks, people listen." And listen they did. For it seems as if a newly formed life insurance company named E. F. Hutton Life was offering a different type of life insurance product called universal life. E. F. Hutton designed these new policies to compete with the more traditional and established whole life insurance policies that dominated the market in 1979.

Universal life was built to be totally transparent, affording the client the opportunity to control the premiums and see the actual charges for mortality and expenses, as well as the interest credited to the policy. The difference between whole life and universal life was not only the total unbundling of the elements of the contract, but the opportunity to receive an interest rate credited at a new money rate. In fact, the first universal life policies were crediting a rate as high as 14 percent. The old whole life contracts were not transparent, other than identifying the reserve basis. The newer and more contemporary universal life contracts laid it all out in black and white. Unfortunately, many agents did not understand the long-term servicing requirements that go with such a flexible product. Since universal life policies are contracts, there must be contractual guarantees. Most companies used a minimum guaranteed interest rate of 4 percent and a guaranteed 1958 CSO mortality table.

THE WILD, WILD WEST

These early versions of universal life were certainly like the Wild West: little regulation, negligible rules, and wide open to almost anything. Agents were telling clients they could pay three or four premiums, and the policy would carry itself to maturity. They also sold policies at a fraction of the old whole life premiums. Simply described, the premium went into a cash value account. Mortality charges and expenses were deducted monthly from the account, prior to the account being credited with the current interest rate. So long as there was a balance in the cash value account, the insurance stayed in force. That's the short explanation of universal life. If the interest credited exceeded the charges, it worked. But, when interest rates started to decrease, the interest credited also decreased, but the charges did not.

Rates that started out at 14 percent soon were on a downward spiral, requiring the insured to deposit increasing amounts of premium into the policies to keep them in force. Many life agents did not properly service their clients' policies, and many clients did not understand the mechanics of the product.

Nonetheless, universal life was rapidly replacing the more traditional and cumbersome whole life policies. Most major insurance companies entered the universal life arena sometime in the early 1980s: "According to a 1981 Life Insurance Marketing Research Association study, 78 percent of the annualized premiums went into traditional cash-value life insurance." By 1985, that percentage was reduced to only 47 percent, with universal life accounting for 38 percent.[9]

Insurance company profitability was severely affected, not only by the draining of cash values from whole life policies but also by the shift to universal life. In order to maintain a comparable level of profitability, the companies had double or triple sales in universal life to equal whole life.

REGULATION

To this point, I have referred to the product as universal life. Although each respective company gave their universal life products unique names, the generic name for universal life is flexible premium adjustable life insurance.

Prior to 1982, the US Internal Revenue Code did not clearly define what constituted life insurance. In 1982, the Tax Equity and Fiscal Responsibility Act (TEFRA) was enacted. This statute provided that a flexible premium contract (universal life and adjustable life) had to meet one of two tests (a cash value corridor test). If the tests were satisfied, then the policies would be treated as life insurance for federal tax purposes. Failure to meet either combination of term insurance and a currently taxable deposit fund had the result of the income on the contract being treated as ordinary income in any year paid or accrued.

With the Deficit Reduction Act of 1984 (DEFRA), a comprehensive definition of life insurance, applicable to all life insurance policies, was established. Essentially, this statute confirms that the basic tests in TEFRA remain.

The premium and corridor requirements under DEFRA are less liberal than those under TEFRA, and apply to contracts issued after December 31, 1984. The more liberal TEFRA guidelines still apply for policies issued prior to January 1, 1985.

Since good things come in threes, in 1988, we had the Technical and Miscellaneous Revenue Act (TAMRA). TAMRA further limited perceived abuses by preventing policyholders from paying large single premiums to purchase life insurance and then borrowing the cash value, tax-free. A policy with premiums in excess of TAMRA limits within the first seven years becomes a modified endowment contract (MEC).

BROKERAGE GENERAL AGENCIES GROW

As universal life became more popular and sales grew, the career companies were slower than other companies to adopt the concept of universal life and develop their own portfolios. Therefore, the bulk of early universal life sales were achieved through independent distribution. This growth in independent distribution created a healthy growth pattern in brokerage general agencies. Companies offering direct contracting in the independent environment soon realized the benefit of adding a common layer between them and the broker. The contracting of BGAs was practical and cost effective.

As the BGA population grew, they formed NAILBA, the National Association of Independent Life Brokerage Agencies. In November of 2010, NAILBA celebrated their twenty-ninth annual meeting. NAILBA member agencies represent 250,000 producers who deliver more than four billion dollars in first-year life insurance premiums annually.

BAND OF BROTHERS AND SISTERS

One of the problems startup BGAs faced in the earlier days was company contracting. Many companies did not want to contract a BGA without a strong sales history or a substantial production commitment, or both. Smaller BGAs were constantly searching for that value-added approach that would give them a one-up on their larger competitors.

With the advent of producer groups (BGAs banding together for contracts, compensation, service, and underwriting), the smaller BGAs could compete in the compensation arena while developing their USPs (unique selling propositions). There are many options available for the broker in the selection of a BGA. If it's only a comp play, with little regard for any kind of value-added service or advanced sales concepting, shopping around will get you a reasonably high payout. But be prepared to wait for a policy to be issued and not to be provided much personal service. You get what you pay for in this world. The same holds true in the BGA world.

As a P/C agency, it's important that you contract with an agency that can provide every service you may need. A BGA that specializes in working with P/C agencies understands your needs, your concerns, and your desires. We understand the importance of your relationship with your clients and the need to provide you with solutions-based marketing, not product sales.

At the Bollinger Group, our USP is "Better relationships start here." We are a concierge agency, catering to our producers' specific needs. We have worked hand in hand with P/C agencies for over thirty years, from marketing development to point of sale. If asked about compensation, our answer is clear and concise: We offer the highest level of compensation possible without sacrificing the quality of the value-added services we provide. Our personalized marketing assistance and our flexibility to fulfill the needs of our brokers and their clients at the highest levels set us apart from those hundreds of other BGAs beckoning for your business.

In the next chapter, we'll examine what you should do, the questions you should ask, and the steps you should follow to build your successful cross-marketing program. The beauty in cross marketing is that no two agencies have to do it the same way.

Marketing plans can range from a simple targeted mortgage protection program to the most sophisticated estate planning, from data mining on the Internet to retirement programs for small businesses. You have the clients, and I'm sure you can think of many other targeted programs that may work inside your agency.

Small agencies, large agencies, personal lines agencies, commercial agencies, bond agencies, marine agencies: you name it, and you can build a marketing program in financial services to increase your bottom line. You can build your own field of dreams. If you build it, they will come!

CHAPTER 11

Summary

Adding true cross-marketing services to your agency's menu of services is a very big step. So many agencies have made a feeble attempt to cross market over the past several decades with little success. They have seen little success for one reason: they were never totally committed to the concept of solutions-based financial services marketing.

How many times have you heard your fellow agents complain that they tried a life person, and he or she ruined a key relationship? Or that he or she stole the clients after their relationship terminated? You may have experienced these problems yourself. Either way, it's my turn to ask you a few questions:

- Did you have a formal contract with the life person?
- Did you introduce him or her to your key clients, and were you present at the initial meeting?
- Did both of you confer on how to approach your clients?
- Did he or she discuss products at the initial meeting?
- Did he or she provide a solutions-based system?
- Did he or she provide his or her selling system to you first?
- Was he or she proactive or reactive?

Finding the right partner is critical to your success in cross-marketing financial services. Chances are you may not have structured the relationship properly. Or you may not have chosen a qualified partner. There are so many reasons to follow some basic guidelines when entering into cross marketing.

A great way to evaluate how well your partnership will work is to test it on yourself. After all, you are a business owner with all the same risk issues as your best clients. After conducting your due diligence, ask your potential partner to provide his or her services for you as he or she would for your clients.

A professional marketing firm should be able to offer you a total package. Although we have focused very heavily on the assisted solutions sale, other parts of the marketing package are also important. Property/casualty agencies should have sufficient data to market to all financial segments of their clientele. Don't ignore those clients who do not qualify for your assisted sale program. Technology is critical. Secure as many personal and business e-mail addresses as you can. There is no more efficient or cost effective way to communicate with your clients than via e-mail.

In addition, insurance companies are developing interactive websites to educate your clients on a multitude of insurance products and concepts. For example, ING offers an interactive, privately labeled site called ING for LIFE. On the site, your clients have the opportunity to learn about the different forms of life insurance and actually build a customized program. If they want to speak with an agent or proceed to the application stage, you'll receive an e-mail. At that point, you have the opportunity to call the client and secure the application online, utilizing electronic signatures. You never have to leave your office!

Also available to the agency is a customized financial services website. Many property/casualty agencies do not properly address financial services on their P/C sites. With your own financial services site, you'll have the ability to provide vital educational information for your clients, give them access to a term quote engine, view product brochures, receive e-mails, web conference, and much more. All this is available for less than fifty dollars per month.

The marketing company should provide the most competitive array of products as well as real-time service. They should be a brokerage general agency (BGA) with a specialty marketing division or have a strong business relationship with a BGA that can offer all the necessary services of a highly qualified firm.

If you really want to drive additional revenue to the bottom line, it's time to make a commitment to financial services marketing. I strongly suggest you start by partnering with a qualified individual or firm. By partnering, you avoid substantial financial outlay and can become functional in a very short period of time. Remember, do your due diligence first. When satisfied that you have covered all the initial steps, *go*! After all, you've had your wake-up call.

(Endnotes)

1. Robert S. Littell and Larry McSpadden, *Crossing the Line: Sales Strategies for Life and Health in the P&C Agency* (Cincinnati, OH: National Underwriting Company, 1997), 16.
2. *Merriam-Webster Online*, s.v. "trust," accessed March 29, 2011, http://www.merriam-webster.com/dictionary/trust.
3. Thomas J. Wolff, *A Trainer's Guide for Capital Needs Analysis* (Vernon, CT: Vernon Publishing Services, 1982), 14.
4. Littell and McSpadden, *Crossing the Line*, 24.
5. John Bartlett, *Familiar Quotations: A Collection of Passages, Phrases, and Proverbs Traced to Their Sources in Ancient and Modern Literature*, 10th ed. (Boston: Little, Brown, and Co., 1919), accessed March 29, 2011, http://www.bartleby.com/100/733.75.html.
6. Peter Drucker, quoted in Patrick J. Below and Bernie Verrill, "A Tribute to Peter F. Drucker: The Sage of Modern Management," CEO Consulting Services, accessed April 11, 2011, http://doczim.com/ceoconsulting/?page_id=69.
7. Derek F. Abell, "Strategic Windows: The Time to Invest in a Product or Market Is When a Strategic Window Is Open," *Journal of Marketing* 42, no. 3 (1978): 21–26.
8. Michael E. Gerber, *E-Myth Mastery* (New York: HarperCollins Publishers, 2005); and Michael E. Gerber, *The E-Myth Revisited* (New York: HarperCollins Publishers, 1995).
9. Ben G. Baldwin, *The New Life Insurance Investment Advisor*, rev. ed. (1994; New York: McGraw-Hill, 2002), 54.